THEN & NOW

FRANKLIN

THE ODELL. The Odell House, also called, among other things, the Webster Hotel, contained a dance hall and opera house and was located on North Main Street where it operated for over 100 years.

FRANKLIN

Elizabeth C. Jewell

*For my family; if not for them I would be lost. For my friends;
I count my fortune in the quality of my friendships and consider
myself very lucky. And for all the history lovers out there, especially
those who became excited at the prospect of this venture!*

On the front cover: **FRANKLIN PUBLIC LIBRARY.** The Franklin Public Library was built in 1907 with an Andrew Carnegie grant and remains a vital and aesthetic part of the community 100 years later. (Vintage photograph courtesy of Franklin Public Library, contemporary photograph by the author.)

On the back cover: **EARLY CENTRAL STREET, LOOKING EAST.** This early-1900s view of Central Street looking east shows the unpaved thoroughfare, including horses with wagons and buggies, the railroad trestle that is just visible at the far end of the street, and an old telephone connection box on the right. (Courtesy of Franklin Public Library.)

Contents

ACKNOWLEDGMENTS

This book would not be possible without the generous assistance of many fellow history buffs and just plain good-hearted folks who have shared their knowledge, interest, and images with me. I am indebted to each of you. To all my friends and coworkers who believe in me; thank you. And thank you to all the new friends and allies I have made during the course of this project, it is unbelievable how truly good people are!

My family has been incredibly supportive and understanding. I am so fortunate. Pat, you still amaze me, thanks for everything you did for making it possible for me to write this book. Thank you Mom, you have been an untiring source of research energy, and Dad, thanks for house-sitting the birthplace this summer. Thank you Jon, for all the emergency writing and photography expertise you have shared over the years. Thank you to my sons; Gabriel, who shares my love of history, and Liam, who has maintained my computer relentlessly. Thank you Alex for defending our country. Thanks to Mandy, my little girl, who shares my belief in magic. Thanks Liam Quinn for directing traffic while I took photographs on Central Street.

I want to thank the staff at Franklin Public Library whom I really appreciate: Rob, Ruth, Sue, and Rachel, you are appreciated. I am grateful to the trustees for access to vital historic materials, also to George for facts pertaining specifically to the library, and Dorothy for entrusting me with her personal image collection. And to the Franklin Public Library itself; happy 100th anniversary!

To fellow residents, neighbors, and history lovers, Jack Benson, Steve Bottomly, attorney Bronwyn-Asplund-Walsh, Delaney Carrier, Tom Charbono, Marjory Cooper, Jo Ellen Divoll, Greg Doyon, Steve Foley, the Franklin Fire Department, Albert Garneau, John Gile, Robert Gile, Deb LaPeirre, Al Larter, Bruce Morrill, Bob Morin, Jim Newton, Morris Salame, attorney Chris Seufert (and Sara and Terry), Stuart Trachy, and Leigh Webb, your assistance and support made this project possible.

A special heartfelt depth of gratitude to the following; Annette Andreozzi, Jim Crowley, Mary Foley, Bob Grevior, Frank Judge, Chris Lewis, Glenn Morrill, Judy Palfry, Nita Tomaszewski, Nancy and Dave Waldo, Zarne and Herb Whiting, thank you for all the time you spent sharing stories and resources with me and helping me to solve the dozens of mysteries that are part of the process.

Thank you Kathi Hennessy, for the inspiration, encouragement, and technical guidance. And thank you Erin Rocha for prompt responses and succinct advice.

All contemporary images were photographed by the author.

I am so glad somebody finally wrote this book!

INTRODUCTION

Whether you are familiar with Franklin or just discovering it, I hope this book reveals a few surprises to you. I have taken well over 1,000 photographs for this book and reviewed at least twice as many old photographs and postcards, thanks to the enormous generosity of several other history enthusiasts. Although I have covered a range of interesting aspects, I have captured only a fraction of Franklin's strong personality.

Franklin, with a population of about 8,000, is the smallest city in New Hampshire. Indeed one of Franklin's charms is having all the conveniences of a city, such as city hall being open every weekday, a selection of banks, and so forth, yet it still maintains a small-town, down-home feel about it.

There are so many layers to Franklin's history that sifting through it all is like undertaking an archaeological dig. I believe to truly understand who we are today, we need to consider where we have been before. Native American settlement remains dot our landscape. Colonial history abides here. We have many wood and brick homes dating from the early 1800s. Farms, foundries, and forges overlap with mills and railroads. All of these played an important role in the development of Franklin's history.

Franklin was established as a town in 1828, quilted together from parcels of four surrounding communities: Northfield, Andover, Sanbornton, and Salisbury. In 1895, Franklin was incorporated as a city comprised of many small regions with a variety of descriptive names, including, Stevenstown, West Franklin, Lake City, Franklin Falls, Paper City, Lower Village, and Webster Place. Webster Place, like other local landmarks, were named after famous New Hampshire orator and statesman Daniel Webster, born in 1792 in Salisbury, now Franklin. His family name graces a homestead, a birth place and associated farms, a family church, and a cemetery, as well as many other local places of historical note.

Situated upon seven rugged granite hills, Franklin has stood the test of time. Two significant rivers, the Pemigewasset and the Winnipesaukee, meet here to form the headwaters of the Merrimack River, which flows south through Massachusetts and empties at last into the Atlantic Ocean. This creates the waterpower source for the great mill towns of Nashua and Manchester, New Hampshire, and Lowell and Lawrence, Massachusetts.

Through producing textiles, paper, lumber, machined goods, and more, Franklin's mills created several wealthy benefactors. They and other town fathers left legacies behind them. Some left their fine estates to be utilized by the City of Franklin for such municipal concerns as a school and a hospital. We have had an inordinate share of entrepreneurs and inventors in Franklin. The names Aiken, Buell, Burleigh, Daniell, Kenrick, Nesmith, Sanborn, and Webster are but a few that live on.

In the early to mid-1900s, the mills faded away. The area struggled to keep its head above the swiftly flowing water. After a slow reawakening, Franklin is emerging now, gracefully looking to the future and respectful of its past.

As a testament to industry, Franklin still has four hydroelectric plants producing power. While many of Franklin's historic buildings have been lost, much of its beautiful old architecture still exists, reminiscent of another era. Most old mill buildings have the additional appeal of elegant architecture and lovely river views from their windows. Historic mill buildings currently house such concerns as a day care, a gym, a furniture business, various studios, an intergenerational center, and luxury apartments. Other mill structures still await creative renovation.

Some mills are gradually aging into vintage ruins. Picturesque mill remains and old aqueduct tunnels in places along the rivers are still visible. Dams continue to spill water where mills no longer operate.

I hope some of the mills and other buildings that stand empty will soon receive another chance. There's a lot of life and promise left in them.

Franklin was once known as the "Gateway to the White Mountains and Lakes of New Hampshire." Until Interstate 93 was built in the 1960s, Route 3 north went right through Franklin, creating a thriving summer tourist industry. Cabins and cottages, inns, restaurants, snack bars, and antique shops lined Route 3 into and out of Franklin. We have a beautiful lake of our own, called Webster of course, and some folks stayed right here in Franklin for their vacations.

Franklin has many internal resources. There is an active historical society, chamber of commerce, opera house, and numerous other community-minded organizations. The city has countless dedicated and compassionate people. The Bread and Roses community kitchen is open to all, giving patrons a gathering place to socialize, and a hot nourishing meal. Our gifted storytellers share their craft with lucky audiences, and a farmers' market brings welcome seasonal color. Our waterways beckon to canoeists and kayakers. Nature trails and historic sites abound.

I know of no other community to hold an annual Class Day Parade. At the close of each school year, all school-age children march, including the soon-to-graduate high school seniors dressed in graduation gowns. They pull the large school bell on wheels, tolling it frequently. The mayor and other city officials, fire trucks, and police cars all intermingle with students from every class in town. The city's residents line the streets and cheer with pride as their youth march by.

Franklin boasts many interesting memorials to our veterans and military personnel. For example: an entire recreation area, including a ski area, is dedicated to veterans. Several monuments and plaques in prominent places and buildings commemorate our veterans' participation in various military campaigns throughout the history of our country. Daniell Park and an adjacent neighborhood, referred to as the Veterans' Project, are in memory of our brave men and women who have served their country. Franklin is also home to Veterans of Foreign Wars (VFW) Post 1698. Franklin has one current and two former armories in town. Small parks are at each end of the Daniel Webster Bridge, one honoring Vietnam War veterans and one honoring Korea War veterans.

While Franklin is rich in natural resources and has its share of architectural and historic gems, I have found the most valuable resource of all is the people. I have never met more compassionate, caring, and generous people anywhere. Thank you Franklin for letting me share your story.

Franklin has come a long way over the years and still has some interesting places to go. Please come along for the ride.

CHAPTER 1

EARLY HISTORY

WHERE WE COME FROM—HONORING OTHERS

THE HOURLY. As the past is understood, the future is revealed. Franklin has strong ties to the past and pays tribute to memorable residents. Franklin is fiercely proud of its veterans and honors them in many ways. This stage, affectionately called the "Hourly," met past Franklin trains unfailingly, delivering passengers to their various destinations.

DANIEL WEBSTER BIRTHPLACE. In 1913, this cabin was detached from the rear of the Sawyer House and relocated on a foundation nearby. Originally it was the home site of Ebenezer Webster and the birthplace of his son Daniel in 1792. The home is furnished as it was in the 1700s and open to visitors on summer weekends. The birthplace is sited in an idyllic country location on the edge of Franklin, in what was once Salisbury.

SAWYER HOUSE AT THE DANIEL WEBSTER BIRTHPLACE. This 1794 Colonial farmhouse is a classic example of an early-American home style. Located at the site of the birthplace and owned by the State of New Hampshire, it is sadly in need of preservation. Since separation from the birthplace cabin, this Colonial has served in a supportive role to that building. Currently, however, it is in such disrepair that it is unused altogether.

ABIGAIL WEBSTER HOUSE. This historic home, originally built for Daniel Webster's sister Abigail around 1805, has been lovingly preserved by a series of devoted owners. During the days when Route 3 north through Franklin was a well traveled tourist road to the White Mountains, this home was a popular inn and restaurant, as shown in the early photograph taken about 1930. It was also an antique shop for a while.

ODELL ARCH. This graceful granite structure has stood at the entrance to Odell Park since 1900. It was named for Herman J. Odell of the Franklin Needle Factory. Odell's widow, Petula Odell, donated the funds for its creation. The area now known as Odell Park was once a Native American settlement. For generations now, it has been a central gathering place for Franklin's residents for picnics, ball games, and other community events.

DUDLEY LADD HOUSE. This graceful old home overlooking North Main Street has a few secrets. It was a very effective player in the Underground Railroad. Franklin lore has it that when the abolitionist family living here was raided in a search for runaway slaves, they sent a young daughter to bed, beneath which several slaves were hidden. The family told the searchers the girl was deathly ill with a very contagious disease. The ruse worked, and the searchers left.

GILE FAMILY HOME, GILE ROAD. This 1804 Colonial-style house was built on 400 acres acquired in the late 1700s by early Gile forefathers. Still in the family and obviously cherished, this lovely homestead has recently been refurbished. While no longer a working farm, this property still abides in a pastoral setting at the rural edge of town. If homes could talk, this one would tell some interesting stories.

FRANKLIN'S FIRST PERMANENT ARMORY. This was Franklin's first masonry armory, built in 1913 on Memorial Street. Although the city mustered in several other temporary locations, this was the first permanent home of Franklin's New Hampshire National Guard. They headquartered here until 1934, when the torch was passed to the second permanent armory, located directly across the street. Today this proud old soldier stands silent sentry at the gateway to Odell Park in Franklin's nucleus.

FRANKLIN'S SECOND PERMANENT ARMORY. Franklin's second masonry armory, completed in 1934, served the city's military needs well. Larger than the first, this multistoried armory contained some nice features, like a large fireplace in the troop's gathering room. Located directly across from the former armory and flanking the other side of the entrance to Odell Park, this structure was rededicated in 1965 as the Henry J. Proulx Recreation Center. The center provides programs for the youth and families of the city year-round.

New Hampshire National Guard Armory
197th Coast Artillery   Battery H
Erected 1933-1934
Franklin, N. H.

Veterans' Project Home. This home was originally the corner store in a development referred to as the Veterans' Project. Following World War II, Hon. Warren F. Daniell donated property, then known as the Old Sands Farm, for this neighborhood. This land includes nearby Daniell Park and house lots for 75 veterans and their families. Streets in this section of Franklin have patriotic names such as Glory, Freedom, and Victory.

COMMERCE

INDUSTRIAL INFLUENCE—MILLS AND RAILROADS

STEVEN'S MILLS DAM. When the mills and railroads ruled, Franklin was a hive of activity. The population boomed and industry flourished. When the mills closed and the railroads faded away, new enterprises settled into the old mills. Disused rails created hiking and snowmobile trails. This dam near the Steven's Mills complex continues to spill water to this day.

ACME KNITTING MACHINE COMPANY. Located on Memorial Street, this former manufacturing facility has had many faces. Once it was a nationally known knitting machine parts producer. Since closing in 1955, this building complex has been home to an artist's studio, an auction storage facility, a newspaper office, a public gymnasium, legal offices, a grocery store, and more. There are still lovely river views from many of the windows of this fine old building.

SULLOWAY MILLS, FLOOD. This photograph was taken at the bottom of River and School Streets. How many of these residents are displaced mill workers thinking "what next?" as they stare despondently at the mill underwater during one of the several floods that plagued Franklin in the past. This mill is now home to a tastefully restored complex of luxury apartments along the river, a fine example of historically sympathetic urban renewal.

MILL STORE, OFFICE. This building, originally built as part of the Sulloway Mills complex, has seen many uses over the years. It is believed to have been office and store space at various times for the mills and most recently was utilized as a video store. It is currently empty. This interesting building is conveniently located on the corner of Central and River Streets.

STEVEN'S MILLS. Most of these brick buildings, arranged in companionable groups, sit between the Winnipesaukee River and Central Street, with a few buildings on the opposite banks nearby. Some of these architectural beauties house current businesses and some still await discovery. Dams and walkways associated with these historic textile mill buildings can still be seen, spanning the river in places.

FRANKLIN FALLS PASSENGER RAILROAD STATION. This station was built in the early 1890s. It was a beautiful example of classic Victorian railroad architecture and sat on the corner of School and Franklin Streets, diagonally across from the present post office. It was razed when the passenger trains ceased to operate here and the brick building, now Verizon, seen in the contemporary photograph was built on the same spot. Residents still reminisce fondly about this station.

FRANKLIN FALLS FREIGHT STATION. The brave lad in the center of this picture is on a small hillock in the midst of the flooded landscape surrounding this railroad freight depot. Despite being a victim of the flood of 1927, this River Street building, located on the banks of the Merrimack River, now stands beautifully restored. Today rehabilitated freight cars linger in the rail yard here, in the shadow of the renovated Sulloway Mills.

RAILROAD COTTAGE HOTEL, RIVER STREET. This surviving example of railroad hospitality demonstrates the impact the railroad had on the fabric of Franklin. Years after the railroads have gone, reminders such as this recall the days when residents set their watches to train whistles and station schedules. This former hotel catered to weary travelers and was conveniently located across from the River Street Station and below the Franklin Street Station. Today it has been restored as an apartment complex.

TOURISM

WHEN FRANKLIN WAS BOTH MEANS AND DESTINATION

Aiken's Point and Summer House,
Webster Lake, Franklin, N. H.
Published by W. S. Stewart

AIKEN POINT. Once Franklin's main road led to the mountains and was lined with tourist cabins, campgrounds, inns, antique shops, and restaurants. Some visitors just visited on the way through and others spent their entire vacations in Franklin. This unusual postcard showcases Aiken Point at Webster Lake through a frame of birch bark.

AIKEN MANOR, WEBSTER LAKE. This beautiful former summer home of the Aiken family is located on Webster Lake at the northwestern edge of town. One outbuilding on the property included a private bowling alley. Originally the Aiken family owned all the property on both sides of the road, as far as they could see from their home, including scenic Aiken point on the lake. Later the manor became a lakeside inn. Now this is a private residence, renamed Aplund Manor.

BIRD'S NEST COTTAGE, WEBSTER LAKE. This cottage home overlooking Webster Lake was once an inn and restaurant from the late 1800s until the mid-1900s. Bird's Nest Cottage catered to the needs of early tourists. The Webster Lake Railroad stop was located conveniently close by. Guests of the inn were shuttled to nearby barn dances in a hay wagon, recalls a Franklin resident who grew up in the cottage.

COTTAGE ROW, WEBSTER LAKE. This section on Webster Lake was referred to on old area maps as Lake City. In 1870, a local icehouse owner built 12 similar cottages on this lakeshore. A stipulation was placed in the original deeds, which continues today in perpetuity, that each owner would not harvest ice from the lake. All 12 cottages on Webster Avenue remain today, some greatly altered and modernized and some retaining their original vintage charm.

DR. LAGACE BEACH, WEBSTER LAKE. This is the Franklin Public Beach located on Route 11 at the southern edge of Webster Lake. It was named for Alphonse Lagace, M.D., a noted and much-loved physician and past mayor of Franklin from 1934 though 1937. Many recent improvements have been made to this section of shorefront, including expanded parking, an updated bathing house, and a boat launch. Note how those bathers just drove their cars right into the lake!

THE GATEWAY INN, SOUTH MAIN STREET. This inn on Route 3 north, also known as South Main Street, reminds one of the days when Franklin was a vacation stopover. Nicknamed the "Gateway to the White Mountains," Franklin's outer limits were dotted with holiday cottages and guest houses welcoming northbound travelers. Interstate 93, built in the 1960s, bypassed the city, and most wayside inns and cottage colonies have disappeared or been reincarnated. This structure now serves as a multifamily home.

ISAAC HALE HOUSE. Isaac Hale was an early settler in the area now known as Franklin. He once occupied this brick Georgian Colonial home built in the early 1800s. Later this house, located on the main route between Concord and the White Mountains, became known as the Gardner Longfellow House. During the halcyon days of the tourist seasons, this home offered camping, lodging, meals, snacks, gasoline, automotive supplies, and general store facilities to travelers. This is now a private residence.

WEBSTER PLACE SCHOOLHOUSE, ANTIQUES SHOP. Originally built of native brick as a schoolhouse in 1815, it served that section of West Franklin then known as the Lower Village. It became a tearoom and antique shop during the days when Route 3 was the main road to the White Mountains. A large enclosed porch was added to the front. The building is now a single-family home being restored to reflect its historic past.

THE DANIEL WEBSTER INN. This grand dame of inns on North Main Street changed hands several times and went by many names over the more than 100 years it operated. A restaurant, dance hall, and opera house were also located at this location. It was finally removed when maintenance became too costly, and now the empty lot provides overflow parking for nearby businesses.

THOUSAND ACRES CAMPGROUND, ROUTE 3. Although the original Colonial-style farmhouse above was once nearly destroyed by fire, it was conscientiously rebuilt. This once thriving farm has been preserved for many additional generations of enjoyment by the creation of a clean and convenient camping environment. Guests include overnight tent campers who prefer secluded sites to seasonal RV enthusiasts craving all the conveniences. Pets are welcome, and nature is abundant.

CHAPTER 4

DOWNTOWN

MUNICIPAL SERVICES AND OTHER UNDERPINNINGS

CENTRAL STREET, 1949 AND TODAY. North Main Street in West Franklin was the original downtown district. Industrialization and expansion eventually created commerce on the east side. Schools and community services followed to the newer Franklin Falls region, which remains the heart of the city. Many of the Central Street buildings in this 1949 postcard remain relatively unchanged today.

CENTRAL STREET, LOOKING WEST. Syndicate Block occupies the right-hand side in the foreground of this old photograph. Continuing westward, note the then recently completed Memorial Hall and the buildings just beyond it. Those smaller buildings occupied the site of the current Franklin Public Library before 1907, when the library was built. Above is Syndicate Block as it appears today.

MEMORIAL HALL CLUSTER. Franklin's public library and opera house/city hall still appear much as they did in this early-1900s postcard. They are still the jewels in Franklin's crown. Dedicated in 1893, Memorial Hall shared space as opera house and city hall. Until shortly after World War II, plays, balls, musicals, and other community events took place here. Eventually the use of the building became more municipal and less cultural. However the tide turned again in 1999 when a movement began to restore the opera house to its former use and glory. Today it is once again the cultural center of the community.

SHEPARD BROTHERS STORE FIRE. The wooden, three-story Shepard Brothers Store, at the corner of Central and Franklin Streets, burned in 1904. The remaining shell was moved to nearby Memorial Street and rebuilt there. A new building was built in brick at the corner location in 1905, occupying the original footprint. In 1923, this became the Holmes and Nelson Building. This corner building is entirely restored today, including tin ceilings and wooden floors. Today it enjoys new life as the Franklin Antique Market, a quality emporium providing an elegant cornerstone to Franklin and Central Streets.

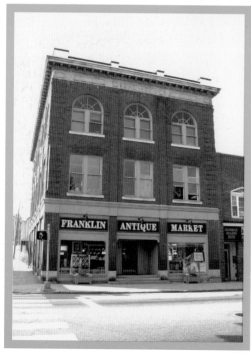

BANK BLOCK, FRANKLIN SAVINGS BANK. The Franklin Savings Bank opened nearby in 1869 with one employee. The main branch, shown below, was built in 1886. The addition at the left and the pink granite trim were added in 1961. Over 138 years later, Franklin Savings Bank has over 100 employees and multiple branches in several surrounding communities. Franklin Savings Bank continues to provide a wide variety of services to customers, with a long tradition of personal service.

GREVIOR'S FURNITURE, CENTRAL STREET. This family-owned business (three generations and counting) has served the Franklin community's furniture needs for 75 years. Located in some of Franklin's carefully restored historic paper mill buildings, Grevior's Furniture continues to offer high quality home furnishings at competitive prices. The Grevior family has generously donated land for the newly created Trestle View Park, next to the furniture store on Central Street. The old photograph below was taken in the 1960s and the current photograph, two fires later, shows the store today.

KIDDER MACHINE COMPANY, CENTRAL STREET. This large building on the corner of East Bow Street was once located across the river from its current location on the site now called Trestle View Park. It was moved several years ago and has since been expanded several times. Today it is the home of Sanel Auto Parts, adjacent to the Sanborn Bridge.

PRE-LIBRARY, CENTRAL STREET. The site of the current Franklin Public Library contained several other establishments before it was built in 1907. Stables, a blacksmith shop, and others shared this site. Before that, local Native Americans hauled fish up to dry on this property, having several weirs in the river behind the current library. Memorial Hall on the right was completed in 1893, so this picture was taken after that but before 1906 when ground was broken for the library construction.

NEW POST OFFICE, FRANKLIN STREET. Previously the post office was in several other locations in East and West Franklin. In 1922, two homes were removed to create space for this imposing, classically designed post office building. When it was built, the busy Franklin Falls Passenger station for the Franklin Tilton Railroad was diagonally across the street. This part of town is much quieter now with the station gone and the post office being the center of activity on Franklin Street.

DANIELL JUNIOR HIGH SCHOOL. The Honorable Warren Daniell Estate sat on a promontory overlooking the headwaters of the Merrimack River. It was given to the school department in 1924 when the impressive mansion home was converted to a new junior high school for the children of Franklin. Further additions were built, and the structure eventually grew to become the city's high school. The mansion portion was torn down in 1939 when it became unsafe and abandoned.

HANCOCK HIGH SCHOOL. When this high school was built in 1876, it could be seen from almost every part of Franklin Falls. Commanding a position high on the hill above Central Street, it finally closed its doors for the last time in 1939. Now the police station and courthouse command this hillside but are less visible because they are not as tall as the old school was and the lot currently has a healthy growth of trees.

SMITH LIBRARY ON CENTRAL STREET. The humble building in this vintage photograph was one of the original library buildings for the city of Franklin, organized in 1880 and serving as library until the present public library was built in 1907. The structure later became St. Jude's Episcopal Church, until it was disbanded in 2002 due to a much-reduced congregation. It now has another significant role in the Franklin community; as the Twin Rivers Interfaith Food Pantry, serving local families in need.

LIBRARY VISTA. This early Franklin Public Library vista, taken at a bend in the Winnipesaukee River, shows the backside of the Acme Machine Company to the left. At the time, the library was covered in ivy. Today the Acme Machine Company buildings are still there, partially in use, and the landscaping around the library has grown up. This is a pretty spot on Central Street in Franklin's busy downtown.

The Hospital, Acme Machine Co., and Public Library from the Winnipesaukee River, Franklin, N. H.

TRESTLE AT NESMITH STREET. When the railroad came to Franklin, it changed much of the local landscape. The slope at Prospect and Central Streets was altered to build tracks and a trestle high above the river. The trestle still stands and remains such a picturesque focal point in downtown Franklin that a nature trail has been developed, following abandoned Nesmith Street and the old rail bed along the river. Trestle View Park was created across the street, obviously in view of the trestle.

NATURAL HISTORY
RURAL REMNANTS,
RECREATION, AND NATURE

ELKINS FARM SITE, RIVER STREET. Franklin has abundant natural resources and history. Native American artifacts and settlement sites, a Colonial fort, and industrial ruins all make for interesting research. Hiking, kayaking, fishing, parks, golf, and more make Franklin a great place to enjoy the outdoors. Shown here in transition, this early farm site became the location of the Sulloway Mills.

FLOOD, FRANKLIN AND GROVE STREETS.
These homes, situated above the Merrimack River, have seriously been affected by the flood of 1936. This event devastated much of Franklin when it occurred. All over town, residents clustered together to wait out the rising water and offer mutual support to one another. This neighborhood eventually recovered from that disaster. Since the construction of an extensive dam system in 1942, residents can feel confident that flooding of that magnitude is truly a historic event.

NATURAL HISTORY

FRANKLIN FLOOD CONTROL DAM SYSTEM. The Franklin Dam, a Pemigewasset River Valley project, was constructed under the supervision of the Boston District Corps of Engineers, U.S. Army Flood Control for the Merrimack Valley. Construction for the $4 million dam commenced in 1939 and was completed in 1942. Before the dam was here, serious annual flooding was always a possibility. Now nature trails and tours are features here.

MOJALAKI GOLF CLUB, PROSPECT STREET. Originally farmland overlooking the Merrimack River and the Ragged and Kearsage Mountain ranges, Mojalaki (a Native American term meaning "carrying place") was developed into a breathtakingly beautiful and challenging golf course in 1921. Over the years, some experiments were attempted with expansion and the course name, but time has proven that the original name and nine-hole plan worked best. An additional newer nine holes have become Mojalaki Golf Academy promoting local and youth golf.

ODELL PARK, CENTRAL FRANKLIN. This park was developed in the late 1800s and early 1900s. It was named for Herman J. Odell of the Franklin Needle Factory. The caretaker's cottage is seen in the distance. The park is actually located on what was once an island in the Winnipesaukee River. In the old photograph, a man is preparing to launch a canoe across the ball field, then under water as the result of the flood of 1936.

OLD NATIVE AMERICAN MORTAR LOT. This collection of Native American artifacts is located on top of what is now called Willow Hill, within a small lot bounded by a stone wall enclosure. A large boulder with a depressed center was used by local Abnaki tribes (this is the spelling as it appears at the lot entrance) and then by early settlers to grind maize. It also contains a boulder with a shad carved upon it. Shad was a native fish, abundant in the area before dams were built on the nearby rivers.

CONNECTIONS
THE PLACES PEOPLE
COME TOGETHER

OLD FREE WILL BAPTIST CHURCH. Franklin has come together for hard times, natural disasters, and celebrations. A lot of strong characters have been built here. Included in this chapter are some popular community gathering places for Franklin residents throughout the years. Before 1914, this structure was a church, and since then it has been many other things.

CONGREGATIONAL CHURCH, SOUTH MAIN STREET. This church was originally built in 1820. It sustained a serious fire in 1902 that destroyed most of the interior, but it was rebuilt faithfully in the original style. It appears today much as it did when Daniel Webster and his family worshipped there long ago. The cemetery, originally situated behind this building, was moved to make way for a rail bed when the Northern Railroad extended its line to Vermont.

MILL WHEEL, TRESTLE VIEW PARK. When one of the large abandoned Steven's Mills buildings burned in a horrific blaze, this fly wheel was salvaged. The 11-ton wheel was part of a steam engine powering the textile mill located across the river from where it now rests. Today it is the centerpiece of Trestle View Park overlooking the Winnipesaukee River, also spanned by the massive picturesque railroad trestle. The river trail begins and kayakers exit at this point. The park is the culmination of the dedicated efforts of many committed Franklin citizens.

Franklin City Hospital, Aiken Avenue. Once the beautiful mansion home of Walter Aiken, overlooking the city of Franklin, this site became a hospital in 1910. For years, the original mansion served as the medical facility and has grown continually since with various additions as needed. Finally when the need for expanded parking prevailed, the old manor was removed altogether. The spirit of generosity and caring that the institution was founded upon, continues today at Franklin Regional Hospital.

62

FRANKLIN PUBLIC LIBRARY INTERIOR. The interior of this distinguished building has changed little in 100 years, technology not withstanding. Large windows bring natural light into the sitting areas and stacks. The floor of the lobby is inlaid marble. Several fireplaces add to the sense of warmth in this beautiful building that beckons residents to enter and read. Palladian windows on the second floor bring daylight into the stage area there. This library is a study in elegant architecture.

OPERA HOUSE PERFORMANCE. Events like this 1916 performance in the historic photograph below were a regular feature of life in Franklin in the days before television. Thanks to the efforts of Franklin Opera House Incorporated and many other dedicated benefactors, the opera house once again has regular theater and concert performances. The current photograph is from the recent *The Sound of Music*. Once again, the stage rings with the talented voices, acting, and music of local talent and special guest performances.

SANBORN HALL, PROSPECT STREET.
This stately carpenter shingle–style home,
built in 1889, served as Franklin's first
hospital. It opened in 1905 under the care
of Dr. John W. Staples and Dr. James B.
Woodman. It continued to serve Franklin, even after the Franklin City Hospital
opened in 1910. It closed in 1913, after
the death of Staples. This home has been
carefully restored and maintained as a
private residence ever since.

FRANKLIN HIGH SCHOOL CLASS, 1904. This Franklin High School 1904 class of 16 serious-looking young adults probably had its class picture taken at the Franklin Hancock High School, on the hill in the center of Franklin Falls. The Franklin High School 2004 class of 104 eager graduates had its photograph taken 100 years later in the gymnasium of the current Franklin High School on Central Street, overlooking the headwaters of the Merrimack River.

GILE'S DAIRY. In 1940, the Gile's Dairy began in a small building atop Willow Hill, where milk was pasteurized for the first time in Franklin. In 1946, the business moved and expanded to include a family-owned dairy bar and grill, soon a choice local gathering spot until the 1960s. For the last several years, this establishment operated as Favorites Restaurant, but sadly that too has recently closed. However, it appears a new eatery will shortly be moving in.

NEW HAMPSHIRE ORPHANS' HOME. The Orphans' Home was established in 1869 for orphans of the Civil War. This property was developed on the former Elms Farm, which had been in the Webster family from 1800 to 1852. Even later in its history, it became the home of the Sisters of the Holy Cross. Most recently, it is undergoing transition after recent acquisition by a local innovative restaurateur and visionary. Fortunately the new owner also understands that respecting and preserving history is good business for everyone, including Franklin.

PEABODY HOME. In 1938, four women, Anna G. Blodget, Mary and Clara Rowell, and Eliza T. Shepard, bequeathed the means to establish a home for the aged in the center of Franklin. The sites adjacent were acquired and incorporated into the current Peabody Home property, which opened in 1942. This property is now a multilevel care facility for seniors and is sited on beautifully landscaped grounds on a bend in the Winnipesaukee River.

Congregational Church Bell. When this bell cracked, it was sent by train to Boston to be recast. The above photograph shows Joey Emery of Andover with his oxen, Star and Swan, bringing the bell back from the station to be reinstalled in the steeple. This same location today, shows the bell in the steeple and the Franklin Academy removed, leaving the parish hall behind.

THE UNITARIAN UNIVERSALIST CHURCH. This elegant half-timber-style structure sets back near a bend in the Winnipesaukee River, right in the center of Franklin. It was built in 1883 for just over $16,000, including the price of the land. In 1927, the building underwent some restoration, including removing its steeple. Today it remains an active church, as well as the home of the community kitchen year-round, and the venue of a local farmer's market in the summer.

INTERSECTION, NORTH AND SOUTH MAIN STREETS. This is where the west end of the Daniel Webster Bridge is anchored. It is a very busy section of Franklin. Once a tranquil thoroughfare, this intersection now contains myriad stop lights and traffic signals. The original narrow two-story house still stands behind all the electronic equipment, although few other landmarks at this location remain unchanged. The original buildings on either side have faded into history.

CHAPTER 7

HOMES AND BUSINESSES

NEIGHBORHOODS AND LIVELIHOODS, PLACES OF INTEREST

WEBSTER LAKE FILLING STATION. Many homes and businesses in Franklin remain in families for generations. Where people live and work becomes part of who they are. Family homes and traditions are still cherished here. In the 1920s, the Dolloffs ran a filling station at Webster Lake, renting rowboats to vacationers and operating a small campground.

Center Chimney Gambrel Cape, c. 1732. This home is not originally native to Franklin. It was built in Rumford (now called Concord) in 1732, carefully dismantled, and moved in 1928 to this site at the southern edge of Franklin where it was meticulously rebuilt in its original form. Each piece was numbered and labeled to make sure that everything fit perfectly back together. This classic New England home retains its original wide-board floors, walls, and hand-hewn beams.

BENSON AUTO DEALERSHIP, NORTH MAIN STREET. The Benson family has been providing quality automotive sales and service for four generations in their expanded North Main Street location. Begun in 1911, Benson Auto is the oldest Chevrolet dealership in America. In 1970, the structure in the original picture was replaced by the building in the current photograph, creating more space. High quality service and customer satisfaction are a tradition at this family business where history continues to repeat itself.

CORNER, EAST BOW AND CENTRAL STREETS. This huge house actually comprises two original structures, joined at some point in the past. In the historic photograph, notice the porches were originally on the front of the house at the left, as it faced Central Street. In the contemporary photograph, the two homes have been combined. This home is now a multifamily apartment complex in a very convenient location at the edge of the downtown area, facing East Bow Street.

HOMES AND BUSINESSES

CORNER, GLORY AND PATRIOT AVENUES.
Shortly after World War II, land was developed into a neighborhood consisting of a park and 75 house lots that were awarded by raffle system to World War II veterans. Each winner paid an extremely nominal sum for his property and received an affordable mortgage. Until recently, many of those plots were occupied by the original owners. The 1950s photograph shows one home during construction. The other shows this inviting home today.

FOOT OF WILLOW HILL. This has been an area of ongoing activity during Franklin's history. Many mills have been located here along the banks of the Winnipesaukee River, as well as numerous other industrial support businesses, taking advantage of the incredible water power. Boardinghouses and other accommodations for mill workers were also located in this vicinity. Most traffic that passes through Franklin today passes this spot near the Sanborn Bridge and the old railroad trestle.

KENRICK FARM, SOUTH MAIN STREET. The Kenrick family was significant in the development of Franklin. For years, a livery was run out of this historic farm, built in the mid-1800s. The main barn and stately home have been restored and continue to be a landmark in the city. Today the property houses a storage facility, utilizing the large barn and outbuildings. Two buildings on Central Street and a park once bore the name Kenrick as well.

Nettie's Place, Summit Street. This gracious home, situated high above the Northern Railroad line and surrounded by gardens, has been lived in and loved by the same family for over a century. Years of memories and emotional treasures, like the child's playhouse used by four generations, fill this homestead. The house is fondly called "Nettie's Place" by the current descendants after a favorite eccentric great aunt who occupied this home for many years. Sometimes she seems to be there still!

NORTH MAIN STREET, CHANCE POND ROAD. In its early days, North Main Street in West Franklin was very busy. The downtown included a post office, stores, businesses, hotels, and homes of noteworthy citizens. Chance Pond intersects the northern end of this bustling section. Chance Pond Road, an area of early Franklin industry, runs the length of the outlet to Webster Lake and had multiple dams, mills, and other water-based industries. At one time, it was the main road to Andover.

OPPOSITE POST OFFICE, FRANKLIN STREET. This section of Franklin Street has seen many changes. Once mostly single-family homes, as in this old photograph, some were removed to make way for the train station built about 1894.

Other homes were removed to make way for the "new" post office. Now the train station is gone, and this area continues to evolve with progress. Many small businesses and professional offices have moved into the restored vintage homes remaining here.

HOME IN AIKEN HEIGHTS. This home, with some craftsman bungalow–like features, was built in the section of town known as Aiken Heights. This land was once owned by Franklin businessman Walter Aiken and was originally part of the Aiken estate, where Franklin Regional hospital currently resides. This home has changed little since it was first built. It is one of several appealing homes in this part of Franklin, located near the Veterans' Project.

SEUFERT LAW OFFICES, CENTRAL STREET. This English Tudor–style mansion is a replica of one seen in England by the senior Alvah Sulloways and built as a wedding gift for their son Richard and his wife in 1914. In 1987, the home suffered a serious fire, and the building remained abandoned for many years. Fortunately the home and grounds were meticulously restored in 1991 and stand testimony to the results of this effort as Seufert Law Offices.

Sulloway Mansion and Barn. Alvah W. Sulloway, wealthy mill owner and significant Franklin businessman, built this splendid home here in sight of his industrial base, near the downtown district but on a side lane overlooking a very picturesque section of the Winnipesaukee River. The location of the Sulloway estate barn is now the site of the local VFW Post 1698.

FEED AND GRAIN, RIVER STREET. This complex of rail-side warehouses and storefront structures is still intact on River Street, and local businesses continue to operate from these renovated buildings. They maintain the original railroad flavor of the old freight yards on River Street and add a fine historic note to this riverside railroad neighborhood that includes the Railroad Hotel across the street.

BROWN'S HILL, NORTH MAIN STREET. This section of town is where the road leads north from Franklin to Bristol, then to the mountains. The Pemigewasset River follows the course of this road and caused the flooding in this early-1900s photograph. The Franklin Dam has been in place for 64 years and provides security to those living near the river. Times have changed and the two homes in the foreground of the photographs have been converted to condominiums, while the house on the right was razed to widen the road.

BOW STREET HOME. This home has been here for many years. It sits directly across from one of the original Steven's Mills, which burned about 10 years ago. It may have been closely connected with the mill during its heyday. It has been well maintained, and although it is on a side street, it is close to all the downtown amenities in Franklin.

OAK STREET HOME. This home was lived in by Napoleon and Florence Durgin in the 1920s. The mother of the lender of this old photograph lived in this house as a child with four siblings. The home is still there, one of several pretty and well-landscaped houses in the neighborhood. Oak Street is off Prospect Street, close to Central Street.

SOUTH MAIN STREET HOME. This was once the home of a Judge Blodgett. It is shown in the older picture shortly after it was built. There are many large old homes in this neighborhood that has seen many changes. At one time, the West Franklin Passenger depot was located nearby. South Main Street is also Route 3 north, and it was a well-traveled route for those heading to the White Mountains and other northern destinations.

HOMES AND BUSINESSES

PLEASANT STREET HOME. This Dutch Colonial home was here when Pleasant Street, once called Leighton Road, was still unpaved and relatively unpopulated. The home has seen some changes over the years, including tastefully closing in the back porch for living space and acquiring many new neighbors. It's a fine home in a beautiful location. Pleasant Street has been paved for many years now.

G. W. GRIFFIN COMPANY. This long brick building shown with these proud employees still stands in the old industrial park on Memorial Street. A variety of saw blades were manufactured here in the late 1800s to the late 1900s. Additions to the structure continued to be added until the 1920s. Since this historic photograph was taken, the roof has been removed, and now the building stands abandoned and waiting for the next metamorphosis.

OLD NEEDLE COMPANY. This building originally housed the old Franklin Needle Company. It has seen many other businesses come and go since then and has had a lot of revisions. A millpond with a dam still exists behind this nice old brick building on North Main Street. Water comes from Webster Lake, through the outlet along Chance Pond Road, then under North Main Street to the Pemigewasset River.

REPUBLICAN BRIDGE, DANIEL WEBSTER BRIDGE. This bridge, spanning the Pemigewasset River and connecting East and West Franklin, has undergone many changes. Once it was a covered bridge and also a toll bridge. More than once, it was ravaged by storms and rebuilt each time. Thousands of cars still cross its span daily. The Republican Bridge was replaced in 1931 by the Daniel Webster Bridge, which was rebuilt again in 1995. Lushly landscaped parks at each end memorialize Franklin's Vietnam and Korea War veterans.

BESSIE ROWELL HOUSE. This Colonial-style house was once the home of the late Bessie Rowell, a beloved teacher and educator. The home has been greatly extended and tastefully remodeled over time. Rowell taught in Franklin for many years. As a tribute to her numerous educational accomplishments, the Bessie C. Rowell Elementary School, built in 1958, was named to honor her.

Across America, People are Discovering Something Wonderful. *Their Heritage.*

Arcadia Publishing is the leading local history publisher in the United States. With more than 3,000 titles in print and hundreds of new titles released every year, Arcadia has extensive specialized experience chronicling the history of communities and celebrating America's hidden stories, bringing to life the people, places, and events from the past. To discover the history of other communities across the nation, please visit:

www.arcadiapublishing.com

Customized search tools allow you to find regional history books about the town where you grew up, the cities where your friends and family live, the town where your parents met, or even that retirement spot you've been dreaming about.